Sing Praises!

illustrated by KATHY MARLIN

The Standard Publishing Company, Cincinnati, Ohio. A division of Standex International Corporation.
© 1999 by The Standard Publishing Company. Bean Sprouts™ and the Bean Sprouts design logo are
trademarks of Standard Publishing. Printed in the United States of America. All rights reserved.
Cover design by Robert Glover.

06 05 04 03 02 01 00 99   5 4 3 2 1

ISBN 0-7847-1047-3

Standard
Publishing
Cincinnati, Ohio

Jesus Loves Me

Jesus loves me, this I know,
For the Bible tells me so;
Little ones to him belong,
They are weak, but he is strong.

Yes, Jesus loves me,
Yes, Jesus loves me,
Yes, Jesus loves me,
The Bible tells me so!

This Little Light of Mine

This little light of mine,
I'm gonna let it shine.
This little light of mine,
I'm gonna let it shine,
Let it shine, let it shine, let it shine.

The Ɓ-I-Ɓ-L-E

The B-I-B-L-E,
Yes, that's the book for me,
I stand alone on the Word of God,
The B-I-B-L-E. Bible!

Rise and Shine

The Lord said to Noah,
There's gonna be a floody, floody.
The Lord said to Noah,
There's gonna be a floody, floody.
Get those animals (*clap*)
Out of the muddy, muddy,
Children of the Lord.

So rise and shine,
And give God the glory, glory.
Rise and shine,
And give God the glory, glory.
Rise and shine and (*clap*)
Give God the glory, glory,
Children of the Lord!

For the Beauty of the Earth

For the beauty of the earth,
For the glory of the skies,
For the love which from our birth
Over and around us lies,
Lord of all, to thee we raise
This our hymn of grateful praise.

For the joy of human love,
Brother, sister, parent, child,
Friends on earth and friends above,
For all gentle thoughts and mild,
Lord of all, to thee we raise
This our hymn of grateful praise.

Jesus Is a Friend

to the tune of "Ten Little Indians"

Jesus is a friend to little children.
Jesus is a friend to little children.
Jesus is a friend to little children.
I want to be like Jesus.

Jesus Loves the Little Children

Jesus loves the little children,
All the children of the world.
Red and yellow, black and white,
They are precious in his sight.
Jesus loves the little children of the world.

Will You Tell a Friend?

to the tune of "Muffin Man"

Will you tell a friend today,
A friend today, a friend today?
Will you tell a friend today
That Jesus is God's Son?

Go, Tell It on the Mountain

Go, tell it on the mountain,
Over the hills and everywhere!
Go, tell it on the mountain,
That Jesus Christ is Lord!

God Is So Good

God is so good,
God is so good,
God is so good,
He's so good to me.

Jesus, Jesus, I Love You

to the tune of "Twinkle, Twinkle"

Jesus, Jesus, I love you,
Teach me all that I should do.
I will talk to you each day,
Follow you in every way.
Jesus, Jesus, I love you,
I'm so glad you love me, too.

He's Got the Whole World

He's got the whole world in his hands,
He's got the whole world in his hands,
He's got the whole wide world in his hands,
He's got the whole world in his hands.

He's got all the little children in his hands,
He's got all the little children in his hands,
He's got all the little children in his hands,
He's got the whole world in his hands.

If You're Happy and You Know It

If you're happy and you know it,
Praise the Lord! Amen!
If you're happy and you know it,
Praise the Lord! Amen!

If you're happy and you know it,
Then your life will surely show it.
If you're happy and you know it,
Praise the Lord! Amen!

Joyful, Joyful, We Adore Thee

Joyful, joyful, we adore thee,
God of glory, Lord of love;
Hearts unfold like flowers before thee,
Opening to the sun above.

Melt the clouds of sin and sadness;
Drive the dark of doubt away;
Giver of immortal gladness,
Fill us with the light of day!

Do Lord, Oh, Do Lord

I've got a home in glory land that outshines the sun,
I've got a home in glory land that outshines the sun,
I've got a home in glory land that outshines the sun,
Away beyond the blue.

Do Lord, oh, do Lord, oh, do remember me.
Do Lord, oh, do Lord, oh, do remember me.
Do Lord, oh, do Lord, oh, do remember me,
Away beyond the blue.

Doxology

Praise God, from whom all blessings flow;
Praise him, all creatures here below;
Praise him above, ye heavenly host;
Praise Father, Son, and Holy Ghost.
Amen.